# The Secret of Baiting Hollow

by

Patricia Clark Smith

Printed in Victoria, Canada

National Library of Canada Cataloguing in Publication

Smith, Patricia Clark
      The secret of Baiting Hollow / Patricia Clark
Smith.
ISBN 1-4120-0051-3
      I. Title.
PS3569.M53784S42 2003      j813'.54      C2003-901375-8

# TRAFFORD

**This book was published *on-demand* in cooperation with Trafford Publishing.**
On-demand publishing is a unique process and service of making a book available for retail sale to the public taking advantage of on-demand manufacturing and Internet marketing. **On-demand publishing** includes promotions, retail sales, manufacturing, order fulfilment, accounting and collecting royalties on behalf of the author.

Suite 6E, 2333 Government St., Victoria, B.C. V8T 4P4, CANADA

| Phone | 250-383-6864 | Toll-free | 1-888-232-4444 (Canada & US) |
| Fax | 250-383-6804 | E-mail | sales@trafford.com |
| Web site | www.trafford.com | | |

TRAFFORD PUBLISHING IS A DIVISION OF TRAFFORD HOLDINGS LTD.
Trafford Catalogue #03-0414      www.trafford.com/robots/03-0414.html

10      9      8      7      6      5      4      3      2

Dedicated with love to my mother,

**Lillian,**

Queen Mother
Of all the land living merpeople,

For her faith, love, encouragement,
And imagination.

Thank you

# The Secret of Baiting Hollow

The drive to the beach seemed endless. The scenery along the Long Island Expressway was a flat uninteresting series of shopping centers, billboards, and developments. As the family car took the Riverhead exit off the expressway, the acres of green potato fields sprinkled with irrigation pipes assured Brigit that she was minutes from Baiting Hollow.

Brigit's eyes followed the straight horizon line of trees along the fields. The sky was blue. Not a cloud was in sight. She knew the beach was just beyond those trees.

As her father turned onto Edward's Avenue, Brigit could smell the salt air. She inhaled deeply. The tree lined road narrowed as it curved and descended through the cliffs. Anxiously, she watched straight ahead, waiting for the moment she would spy the beach.

As the car took the last curve, the bright blue sky, clear vast waters of the Long Island Sound, and the massive cliffs suddenly appeared.

Nestled at the foot of the cliffs were two rows of cottages on either side of the dirt beach road. The car followed the road as it slightly dropped from Edward's Avenue onto the beach road.  The tires hummed as they hugged along the sandy road.

Aunt Agatha's bungalow was the third cottage on the right.  The car stopped in back of the small wooden cottage on stilts. Brigit rolled up the cuffs of her blue jeans, took off her sneakers and socks, opened the car door, and hopped out onto the sand. "Ouch!  That sand is hot," she said to herself.

Brigit ran straight under the bungalow where she was sure the shaded sand would cool her parched feet.  There she paused and then walked under the front porch.

It was high tide.  The waves splashed white foam just a few feet away from the front porch steps.  As the waves receded, small brown and green seaweed curled around the brightly colored stones on the beach.  Another strong wave pounced back over the rocks, then slid back down the beach.

Brigit tiptoed over the hot sand to the water.  As the next icy wave rushed over and then away from her bare white ankles, her feet sank into the sand.  The rhythm of the water and sand seemed hypnotic.

Brigit walked along the high water mark down the beach.  The slate gray jetty interrupted her downward gaze.  Up and over the stonewall she climbed.

On the other side of the jetty, Brigit

turned and looked at Baiting Hollow. The twelve cottages were nestled on a small, clean, white sandy beach. Black-eyed Susans dotted the tall marsh grass at the edge of the sand. Small birds flew in and out of the marsh. The thick tree-covered cliffs seemed like a fortress, a fortress protecting a small quiet white beach from the hurried, flat, crowded world outside. Being back at the beach filled her with joy.

Brigit's senses were filled with the late afternoon view of the water, the smell of the salt air, and the sound of the waves. At twelve years old she felt an overwhelming call to the sea. Before helping her family open the shutters on the porch or putting

her clothes in the dresser and closet, she
grabbed her bathing suit, jumped into it, ran
out the front door across the sand and
stones to the water, and dove in.

Under water, surrounded by the cold
salty sea, Brigit became part of a quiet,
secret world.  A school of minnows swam by
and a little crab scurried past as seaweed
floated over beach stones and seashells.
And, time stood still.  Unable to hold her
breath any longer, she surfaced, "Whew!"
She floated, dove under again, then swam
back and forth between the jetties:  first the
crawl, then the backstroke, the sidestroke,
and the breaststroke.

The sun was setting.  Orange, pink

purple colors washed across the evening sky and the sound. Brigit thought to herself that she was once again seeing the miracle of nature's everyday masterpiece. Engulfed in the quiet, solemn, stillness of the air and the gently rhythm of the ocean, she watched the sun set below the horizon. The sea and the sky become one.

Silently floating, a speck upon the now dark ocean, Brigit felt a sense of peace only found in the quiet of nature, a goodness so pure she thought, I must be outside heaven's door." And, just when she thought she had reached nirvana, the stars came out: a bright, dazzling, sparkling, twinkling star show.

Walking back to the bungalow Brigit wondered, "I am not sure how long I stayed in the water. At the beach, time does not matter."

That night Brigit slept on the front screened-in porch of the bungalow. She fell asleep to the sound of the waves and the sight of the stars. And, the rhythm of the ocean rested in her heart once again.

******

Morning at the beach is the brightest part of the day. Up at sunrise to the cries of the seagulls and the rippling of the waves at low tide, Brigit stepped out onto the front deck. After a deep breath, she surveyed the beach and then the water sparkling in the morning sun. Two swans and a small cygnet were floating near the jetty in front of the bungalow. How very honored Brigit felt to have such a royal, elegant family say good morning to her.

Brigit's mother, Lillian Twomey Clark, and her Aunt Agatha Twomey Meyer brought breakfast out onto the front porch to the family: orange juice, toast and jam, and the snack pack cereal of their choice. As she sat and talked with her sister, mother, father, two cousins and aunt, Brigit spied the dolphins, pointed, and yelled, "Look!"

She always seemed surprised at the

wonder of these beautiful creatures swimming right in front of the beach. Up and down, in and out of the water they would swim as if in some well choreographed ocean dance. Within their dance sometimes they looked like ancient mermaids. Brigit thought, "Were they trying to communicate with us the way human dancers do?"

That morning her beach friend, Kevin O'Connell, was visiting the family during breakfast. They watched the dolphins together. Kevin said they should get a closer look. So, Brigit and Kevin ran outside and carried his small motorboat to the water. They drove it out to where the dolphins were swimming. When the boat arrived at the school of dolphins Kevin turned off his motor. The dolphins came right up to the boat. There must have been eight or nine of them, a family perhaps.

Brigit whispered to Kevin, "I will never forget this awesome and wonderful moment." Kevin whispered in Brigit's ear, "We have crossed over into another world of these gentle sea mammals, these smooth, graceful gray protectors of the sea." After a while, the dolphins swam away. Kevin started the motor and headed back to the beach.

When the little boat scraped along the shore, Brigit noticed her mother waving and calling to her. She told Kevin she had better go back to the bungalow, that her family was going up to the Twomey farmhouse for the Fourth of July picnic with Aunt Mame and her brother, Uncle David. They would be back around dusk for the fireworks on the beach. "Let's have a bonfire tonight," Kevin suggested. "I'll collect driftwood and pile it in the front of your Aunt Agatha's bungalow the way we always do."

That sounded like a great idea. "Can we go for a swim out to the raft and watch the sunset, too?" Brigit asked. Kevin smiled and nodded as they pulled the boat above the high water mark.

"See you later," Brigit yelled while running to the bungalow. It was such a beautiful day. She loved her Mom, her Dad, and sister and looked forward to seeing her relatives at the farm. In her heart of hearts though, she wanted to spend her first day of vacation at the beach with Kevin O'Connell.

The O'Connell family lived at the beach all year round. Kevin knew every nook and cranny of Baiting Hollow's beach, creek, marshes, and cliffs. He even knew secret trails into the boy scout camp. At least once every summer, Kevin would lead the beach kids down to the creek, across the marsh grass, through the trails, and into Camp Baiting Hollow.

Six or eight kids would quietly follow Kevin through the woods, along a narrow trail near the top of the cliff.  As they approached, they would look down onto the lake and buildings of Camp Baiting Hollow and watch the boy scouts taking swimming lessons, archery lessons, or playing baseball. One of the scouts would always notice and yell, "Beach kids in the camp!"  The scouts would gather like ants as they marched up the cliff.  At the same time, Kevin would turn and lead the beach kids running barefoot as fast as they could through the marsh grass, across the creek, over the rocky beach until they collapsed in front of the bungalows.

The kids would laugh and laugh watching all the boy scouts on the other side of the creek waving their arms and yelling for the beach kids to stay out of their camp. Kevin assured everyone they were safe, because he knew the boy scouts were not allowed to cross over the creek.

******

Brigit enjoyed the day at the Twomey farmhouse picnic with her relatives, but she could not wait to return to Baiting Hollow. That evening she helped her mother carry bags of bowls and baskets of picnic leftovers into the bungalow. Dropping them on the kitchen counter, Brigit ran to her bedroom to slip into her bathing suit, then through the front door, and out onto the front steps.

She saw Kevin sitting by the bonfire he had built. He looked up and waved her down to join him. She bounced down the steps with her beach towel waving in her hand behind her. Brigit walked to the bonfire and stood next to Kevin. The sand felt cold on her bare feet, and the air had a cool breeze. "Are we going for our swim to the raft?" she asked.

Kevin stood up and smiled, "You are such a fish." He took off his sweatshirt, scooped Brigit up in his arms, ran to the water's edge, and threw her in. He dove in and surfaced right next to her. The sound was vast, dark, and warm at night. Without saying a word, the two beach kids started swimming. The pattern of their strokes, hand over hand, and their deep breathing in and out, seemed to mimic the pattern of the waves.

When they reached the raft, Kevin hopped up, then extended his hand to help Brigit up. There was a chill in the air. They could see their bonfire on the shore. The two friends of summer turned and sat shoulder to shoulder looking out at the dark waters of Long Island Sound. They could see Connecticut's lights on the horizon.

"Look at the fireworks on the cliff," Kevin said. Propelled off the cliffs, rockets would burst with a bang into thousands of lights and fall into the sound. Over and over in all sorts of colors and shapes. This summer's fireworks seemed more exciting than ever. They o-o-o'ed and ah'ed as each new explosion of colored lights filled the night sky.

As the last of the fireworks ended, Kevin suggested they swim into shore and enjoy the bonfire for a while. Although content to stay out in the water, Brigit could see Kevin was trembling from the cold and his lips were turning blue.

In unison, they dove into the water and swam back to the beach. Kevin ran ahead and grabbed his sweatshirt and brought Brigit's beach towel to her. He wrapped it around her, and they both ran to the bonfire.

The bonfire was roaring now, blazing high over their heads. Brigit's sister, cousins, and a few beach kids were roasting marshmallows on sticks. Brigit and Kevin joined them. The bonfire warmed them to the bone, and in a very short time they noticed their suits were dry. When the marshmallows were gone, the others seemed to have had enough, said goodnight, and went into their bungalows.

The beach was dark now: no street lights, no house lights. Red embers were all that was left of the bonfire. The stars and the moon were out. In the dark, quiet, coldness of the beach, Brigit wondered out loud, "Why is it Kevin? What is it about this little beach? The minute I see it, the minute my feet sink in the warm sand, the minute I dive deep in the cold salt water, the minute I am with you, I feel happy. I have to wait the entire school year to come back to Baiting Hollow. So, for two weeks out of the fifty-two weeks of the year, I am totally happy. Why Kevin?"

There was a long pause, a long silence. Brigit and Kevin stared at the bonfire embers. She really didn't expect an answer. She knew there was no answer. Her family lived in Connecticut, now just a few flickering lights on the horizon. Baiting Hollow was her family vacation place for two weeks out of the year. Her best friend lived there. That was that.

She was almost ready to accept it, when Kevin took in a long deep breath and then exhaled a long slow painful exhale. Brigit felt terrible. She thought she had upset him. She never saw him annoyed with her before. After another long silent pause, Kevin spoke, "I will tell you the secret."

"What secret?" Brigit asked.

"Please, Brigit, don't interrupt," he scolded. "One evening this past spring, before any of the summer families arrived, I was sitting on the jetty, the one between our families' bungalows, just fishing the way I do every evening. My mother came out and sat next to me. She started to talk about being the last of the original Baiting Hollow beach people who lived here all year round. She reminisced about the good old days. She remembered her mother's stories of the bungalows being built, and she could still name each and every one of the original owners. She loved Baiting Hollow and wanted to know how I felt about it and if I planned to live here forever."

"When I assured her that Baiting Hollow always was and always would be my home, she told me the secret of Baiting Hollow. She had never told another soul, not even my father. I had to promise to only pass the secret on to one person in my lifetime. I had to be sure that special person loved Baiting Hollow the way she and I did.  This was the only way the secret of Baiting Hollow would be safe."

"I believe you are that person.  You must promise to only tell one person in your lifetime.  Can I trust you with the secret of Baiting Hollow?"

Brigit did not know what Kevin was talking about.  She felt a little frightened.  It was dark, they were alone now on an empty beach, and she did not like ghost stories.  Kevin seemed to be in a very strange mood.  She had never seen him like this.  She nodded with her eyes closed and promised, "Yes, Kevin, I do love Baiting Hollow and would

23

never divulge the secret.  I promise I will only tell one person in my lifetime, one person I believe loves Baiting Hollow the way we do and will keep the secret."

Kevin looked away.  He seemed to survey the water for a clue, a sign, or a place to begin.  His eyes rested on the jetty, and he began to tell his story.

\*\*\*\*\*\*

*In a time before time was conceived of, in a place not recorded on maps, off the shores of a ragged coastline, tiny merpeople emerged from the sea.  These beautiful ocean creatures, half fish and half* human, they say, were pronounced the lords and the ladies of the vast deep blue and green sea.

The order and harmony of sea life were perfect. The seaweed and kelp were their food. Their friends were the whales and the dolphins. With seals and seahorses they played.

Mermaids and mermen had babies. Their families were happy and safe. Their friends and their food in the ocean were celebrated and honored by all.

At sunrise, young mermaids would gather on the beach at the edge of the sea. They would laugh, and they'd talk of their future and wonder what it would be. Would *they meet a merman and marry? Would they have children, a family to raise? Would they serve as a priestess or lady for the ocean's royal enclave?*

*Now, Abigail Twomanno was married to High Lord Lahranno of the sea. Evenings after her babies were sleeping, she swam to the shore, sat on the rocks by the sea, and admired its peace and its beauty. Quietly, she watched as the sun set in the sea: orange, purple, and pink. Abigail was content with her home and loved the merpeople of the deep.*

*Engulfed in the quiet, solemn, stillness and the gentle rhythm of the waves, she suddenly noticed some strange forms on the* horizon. She wondered what they could be. They weren't the whales or the dolphins. They couldn't be a coral reef. They weren't a mirage or a shadow. Could they be the human death dragon ships headed for their beach?

Abigail dove into the ocean and swam quickly to her home. She told her husband that the human death dragon ships were near.

Lord Lahranno knew from his father the tales of these gigantic sea cruising ships with evil people who pilfered the deep ocean treasures and captured mermaids for slaves.

Fear struck the heart of Lord Lahranno, "Code Red!" He ordered all merpeople, "Abandon your homes in the ridges. Dive to the deep ravines in the ocean. There you will find sanctuary for your families."

Abigail grabbed her two babies from the cradles where they were peacefully sleeping. She wrapped them in their royal sea sacques then quietly and quickly left. She left their beautiful sea castle in the ridge along the seashore. She held tightly to her tiny sea babies as she swam to the deep hideaway. There she left her babies in their grandmother's care.

The ocean was turbulent. Thousands of merpeople were fleeing, exiled from their

homes. Abigail could see the ships'
silhouettes on the surface of the water above
them.

Abigail swam back to the seashore and
tried to distract the ships the way she had
heard her grandmother say she did many
years ago. She climbed up onto the huge
rocky outcrops and began to sweetly sing and
pretend to laugh as she combed her long curly
red hair.

The death dragon ships headed toward
her. The seamen were lured by her beauty
and song. This magnificent brave mermaid
stayed calm through the death dragon storm.

Suddenly, one of the ships crashed on
the rocky seashore. Abigail watched as the

29

*waves pounded and broke its brittle wooden hull and masts, and the ebb tide washed the debris and the men away.*

*With the loss of one of the ships, the other ships turned and retreated. The mermaid rejoiced at the death dragon's defeat. She was proud to have frightened the ships away. Now, the merpeople could return to their homes in the ridges along the seashore.*

*As she arrived at the deep ocean hideaway, a merpeople meeting was being held. High Lord Lahranno was speaking to the frightened community. He spoke to the merpeople of his lineage, his reign, and his royal inheritance to protect the merclan,*

"We will stay deep in the ocean, away from the beaches and land, away from the sun which makes our scales glisten and our skin freckle, away from the salty sea air." He raised his royal scepter and commanded, "Dive deeper and swim farther away from our former homes which are now unsafe. The merpeople will no longer risk their lives by living near the shore."

Abigail was worried. She knew the merclan could not survive living in the deep dark ocean. They would all surely shrivel and die. Her grandmother told her mother, and her mother made sure she knew:

The mermaids' and mermen's spirits need the water to swim, live, and play. They *also need the sunshine to renew their hearts and minds. Zeus made mermaids and mermen full of beauty and joy, wise protectors of the earth, the sea, and the sky. He made them half fish and half human to ensure the balance in nature. He made the bird, the butterfly, and the dragon fly earthly cousins to the seahorse, sand dollar, and snail who live in the sea. So, whenever you see a sunrise, a sunset, or a blue moon, whenever you hear the waves crash or smell the heather in bloom, you will hear in the distance the mermaids' swoon.*

*Mother told Abigail another one of Grandmother's stories. The day will come when, once again, a merlord will reign with fear to control the merpeople. Millions of years ago when the land rose up out of the sea, the merpeople panicked, and Oysteranno, the First, ordered them to flee from their homes. He had overthrown his elderly merparents, King and Queen Twomanno of the first merclan. The merpeople's exile almost caused them extinction, but King and Queen Twomanno, ancestors of yours, knew this was wrong. They knew the mermaids and mermen were blessed and empowered by Zeus to protect the beauty and peace of the Earth.*

*So, they left their family and community to ensure their family's destiny. They traveled for many years searching for a perfect home. And, they found our beautiful ridge along the rocky seashore. There they had two daughters, Twomey and Troianno. Zeus honored King and Queen Twomanno for their wisdom and bravery by making their two daughters sea goddesses.*

*Abigail stayed still. Within the silent, still darkness of the sea, the ancient courage of her ancestors rose within her, and she knew what she had to do.*

*Abigail had to find the ancient box her mother kept which had been passed through centuries and generations of the Twomanno Clan from Queen Twomanno in case of such a time.*

*Abigail's heart was racing. She*

promised herself she would be brave.   She
gathered up her babies and fled to the ridge
by the seashore.

Deep within the walls of her mother's
home in the ridge, she found the ancient coral
box from Queen Twomanno.   After prying,
pounding, and wrenching, the lid flipped off
the box.   There were two smooth, pink pearls
and a note within the box.

The mermaid floated speechlessly
staring at this awesome, ancient sight.   Then
she picked up the note, opened it, and read in
the lost language of the Twomanno Clan, the
note Queen Twomanno, herself, had written:

These are the Pink Twomanno Pearls.
The power of these Pink Twomanno Pearls

35

*bestow on all Twomanno merpeople the ability to read and understand this message.*

*If a mermaid or merman descendent of the Twomanno Clan believes they are in danger due to the tyrannical control of a fearful lord, these pearls will provide the power to find safe passage to become human and to live on land. Always remember, your destiny to protect the beauty and peace of the Earth remains yours in the sea and in your human form on the land.*

*The ancient goddesses of the sea, Twomey and Troianno, delivered this message and the pearls to me, their Queen mother, from Zeus. Zeus arranged with the dolphins that they would provide the safe* passage of any mermaid or merman who possessed one of these pearls. The Twomanno Pearls are yours. Follow in the path of the other Twomanno merpeople who have used the Twomanno Pearls to find passage into the human world to fulfill their destiny.

First, you must go to the dolphins. Show Queen Daphnia of All Dolphins the Twomanno Pearls. She will assign a dolphin to accompany you to the passageway onto land. Swim fast, swim far, swim long, swim hard, do not stop. There is only one passageway to land. The dolphin will follow the ancient Beluga Current that flows to the coast. Follow the coast heading south. The dolphin will swim with you into the sound

*just north of a narrow but long island. The
dolphin will guide you to a small beach
protected by tall cliffs. The cliffs form a
fortress to protect this small beach hollow.
There are twelve little bungalows at one end
of the beach. The dolphin will leave you by
the second jetty near the third bungalow. As
you touch the land while holding the pearl.
You will take human form. The little gray
bungalow stands on stilts with a small front
porch. A Twomanno descendent will be
watching for you. The dolphin's dance will
alert her to meet you there. Show her the
Twomanno Pearl, and she will provide
sanctuary and safe passage into the human
world.*

*Trust in your spirit, in the spirit of the Twomanno mermaids, and the two great goddesses of the sea, Twomey and Troianno, from whom all Twomanno mermaids are descendent. The time has come to fulfill the second half of your destiny by becoming human.* Abigail sat motionless, speechless, and numb for hours. Startled by the silhouette of another ship overhead, she whispered to herself, "The ancient stories about mermaids joining the human race are true."

Holding her merbabies in her arms and the two Twomanno Pearls in one hand, she decided to use the two pearls for the safe passage of her son and her daughter into the *human world.*

Brigit interrupted again, "Kevin, what does a mythical story about mermaids and mermen have to do with my love of the beach?"

Kevin snapped, "Just listen, and you will understand."

Kevin continued his story, "*Overwhelmed by the message from Queen Twomanno about the beautiful Twomanno Pearls, her worry about her babies, and the possible extinction of the merclan, Abigail knew she had to follow the directions which Queen Twomanno had writtencenturies ago. With sea grass she tied one pearl around each baby's neck, tucked them within their* royal sea sacques, and swam as fast as she could to Queen Daphnia who lived north of her merclan's ridge.

Arriving at the outer banks of Queen Daphnia's castle, she was greeted by a dolphin tending to the castle gardens. Abigail told the dolphin that she had come to see the Queen. The dolphin told her to follow him, and he would take her there.

He swam straight to the Queen's castle. She was so pleased to see Abigail. Queen Daphnia told Abigail that many years ago her mother had brought her to the castle to be introduced to the Queen. Abigail told Queen Daphnia of the trouble among the merpeople. Queen Daphnia knew about Queen

*Twomanno's letter and the precious Pink Twomanno Pearls. There was no time to spare. The Queen called for her swiftest and most powerful dolphin, Daniel, and seven of her best Guardians to escort Abigail and her babies to the mermaid passageway and sanctuary with humans on land. Abigail held onto her babies with one hand and held onto Daniel with the other.*

*Queen Daphnia blessed Abigail, her two babies, Daniel, and the seven Guardians; waved her royal cape; and sent them on their way, "Safe trip, my dear sea creatures."*

*Daniel, with Abigail and her babies, and the Guardians on either side, swam the* ocean day and night. He followed the ancient Beluga Current which he knew would bring him to the sound just north of the narrow but long island Queen Twomanno's letter had directed them to.

As they entered the sound, Abigail noticed the dolphins fell in a line formation behind Daniel. Throughout their sea journey they swam on either side of Daniel, usually below the surface, only occasionally rising above for a breath of air. Now, Daniel was leading the Guardians in a magical sea dance, "Hold on Abigail. Hold on to your babies and to me."

Daniel leaped high out of the water, his smooth gray body seemed to almost suspend in air for a moment, before he dove gracefully back into the sea. After a moment or two he did it again, and again, and again, and again. The seven Guardians followed in suit. Abigail had never seen anything so beautiful as this dolphin dance.

Distracted by the dance, she did not notice that Daniel was approaching land. Suddenly Daniel and the Guardians stopped the dance and continued underwater toward the small beach nestled among the giant cliffs.

When they surfaced for air, Abigail saw twelve little bungalows on stilts in a row on the beach and several dark gray jetties lining the beach. She took a deep breath.

She told Daniel that she was thrilled they found the merpeople's safe passageway for her two babies but also felt great sadness that she would be handing over her babies to a stranger.  Perhaps she would never see them again.  Daniel assured Abigail that she was doing the right thing, "The merpeople under the rule of High Lord Lahranno will certainly perish if they stay deep beneath the sea.  Your children will not only be safe with the Twomanno descendants, they will be able to continue the mermaid and mermen legacy to bring beauty and peace to this planet, Earth."

"You, my dear Abigail, may stay and live with the dolphins.  Queen Daphnia told

45

*me to tell you, that she would like you to be
the teacher of dolphins. The dolphins are
beautiful, strong, brave, and good. For them
to be wise, they must learn more and develop
an understanding of the Earth that only you
can give them. You will be their greatest
teacher."*

*Abigail smiled. She hugged her babies
tightly. "Abigail, you will not only teach the
dolphins, you will swim with us. Every time
we bring an orphaned merbaby to this
passageway, you will accompany us to care
for the baby on the journey. You will see your
babies. They will be among the other Baiting
Hollow beach children. You will know them
by their sparkling deep sea eyes,*

*their sun streaked hair, and their freckled skin. Their smiles will be that of the gods and goddesses. Your children will swim in the morning, during the day, and at night. Their gaze will be toward the sea, for they will always unknowingly long for their mother."*

*Abigail was ready. It was just after sunset as Daniel and the Guardians swam up to the jetty by the third bungalow. Abigail could see the silhouette of a human standing on the front porch of the third bungalow. Her heart pounded. She let go of Daniel for the first time since they left Queen Daphnia. Abigail swam the last few feet to the jetty with her babies.*

*Abigail sprung up out of the water and sat on the jetty with her babies. As tears flowed from her own deep sea eyes, she checked to make sure that one Twomanno Pearl was with each baby. As she opened each baby's sacque, she saw that the Pink Twomanno Pearls had magically turned her babies into their human forms. Their smooth skin, sun streaked hair, deep sea eyes, and cute little smiles captivated Abigail. She hugged her babies and kissed them on their foreheads.*

*Abigail looked up to see the beautiful woman walking toward her. The woman smiled. She had a freckled face and long wavy auburn hair. Abigail knew she must be one of the good Twomanno descendants. The woman stopped by the jetty near Abigail, "Abigail, I am Lillian Twomey, daughter of Margaret Twomey, great, great, great grand daughter of Queen Twomanno. My mother shared the secret of the Pink Twomanno Pearls with me. Now, I greet the mermaids as my mother did for many years. I take the merbabies, now in human form, and promise love and sanctuary for all Twomanno babies. I promise your babies will be safe. The women of the Baiting Hollow beach people have secretly taken care of Twomanno descendants for many, many years."*

*Abigail kissed her babies one more time. And, with one more hug, she handed*

Patricia Clark Smith

*them to Lillian. Through her tears, Abigail watched Lillian take her babies, hug them, then kiss them in the same way Abigail had.*

*Abigail knew her babies were safe, but she would miss them forever. She suddenly noticed another woman walking from another bungalow on the other side of the jetty. Abigail thought she had better leave. So, she dove back into the sound, reached out, and grabbed hold of Daniel, "Good job, Abigail," Daniel assured her. "Now we are heading back to Queen Daphnia. Hold on, sleep tight, I will take care of you."*

*Abigail looked around her and saw the seven Guardians smile at her. She smiled back and hugged Daniel. As he took a leap out of the water, Abigail turned to look back one more time at Baiting Hollow. In the moonlight, on that small little beach, by the jetty next to the third bungalow, she saw Lillian hand one of her babies to the other woman. Abigail knew Lillian's promise was good. Her children would be safe and loved.*

"Lillian? Margaret Twomey? Kevin, what are you talking about?" Brigit demanded.

"The secret that my mother told me, is the secret your mother told her. That night, twelve years ago, Abigail gave her two babies to Lillian. My mother was one of the trusted Baiting Hollow women. Lillian gave Abigail's baby boy to Agnes O'Connell, and she kept

Abigail's baby girl for herself. Agnes named her son Kevin, and Lillian named her daughter, Brigit."

"That's impossible! You're crazy! I know the story of my birth. I have a birth certificate from Southampton Hospital," Brigit said half laughing at Kevin's outrageous story. "Mom was staying with her sister, Aunt Mame. Daddy was going to be away with the Army for months."

"That's right, Brigit," Kevin agreed.

"Mom was so sick and thin that no one believed she was pregnant."

"That's because she wasn't," Kevin explained.

"Yes, she was!" Brigit insisted.

"Anyway, Mom said the labor was so fast and furious, she delivered the baby at the farmhouse where she was staying with Aunt Mame, the way most Twomey children had been born. Mame drove Mom and me to Southampton Hospital to meet Dr. Murphy."

Kevin added, "She had to get you to the hospital for a legal birth certificate as fast as possible. Dr. Murphy was one of the Baiting Hollow beach people and a very well respected doctor in Calverton. He knew the drill."

Brigit, now confused and a little subdued, added, "Mom said that Dr. Murphy told her I was born with a veil, but he didn't save it. He said that seamen would pay

53

thousands of dollars for the veil, because it was believed that the veil had magical powers to protect ships and guide sea captains on their voyages." No sooner had these words come out of her mouth that she gasped, "Oh my goodness! Is it true?"

Kevin nodded, "The royal sea sacques resembled a sheer translucent membrane, a veil over the baby. That is how Lillian and the other Baiting Hollow adoptive mothers let Dr. Murphy know another merbaby made safe passageway into human life. Dr. Murphy made sure that the babies were lawfully registered at Southampton Hospital. Since many women in this area gave birth at home, there was no question of your mother's arrival at the hospital with a newborn baby. He kept no private records of the merbabies who passed through Baiting Hollow. The adoptive mother kept the Pink Twomanno Pearl and the secret which, by decree of Queen Twomanno, could only be told to one special person."

"My mother, Agnes O'Connell, wanted me to someday tell you, because Lillian, your mother, had used her one secret to tell my mother and therefore could never tell you. Lillian wanted you to know your legacy."

Kevin and Brigit sat in silence. It was so dark and cold. Kevin got up, grabbed a bucket from under the bungalow, and walked to the water's edge. He came back and dowsed the charred driftwood with salt water.  He did it two or three more times.

Brigit was so puzzled.  "Are you
kidding, Kevin?" she playfully asked.  (He
could be such a tease.)  Kevin just shook his
head and walked away into the dark night.

******

Brigit tossed and turned all night long.
Her mind reeled with questions about the
story Kevin told her by the bonfire that
evening.  Were Kevin and Brigit the son and
daughter of the mermaid, Abigail?  Was
Lillian Brigit's adoptive mother?  Did Lillian
have one of the Pink Twomanno Pearls?  Was

she one of the Twomey descendants who greeted mermaids at the jetty, received their merbabies, and promised sanctuary for them?  Brigit knew her mother could not and would not tell her even if she asked.

Unable to sleep, Brigit got up and walked out onto the front deck.  She could see the first light, a crack of dawn on the eastern horizon of Long Island Sound.  This sliver of light was an early morning ritual at the beach, morning reveille perhaps.  Tiny marsh birds started to chirp, a flock of seagulls flew off the eastern cliffs, and Brigit watched three fishermen back their boat into the sound and head out to sea.  "Today," Brigit was determined, "I will find out whether Kevin was telling a story or the truth."

As she walked back into the porch, David and Albert, Aunt Agatha's sons were putting together their fishing gear. "You are up early," Brigit commented. "Where are you going?"

"We're going to take the boat across the sound to Connecticut today. We have to get an early start, because we really don't know where we are going or how long the ride will take," David said, informing his mother for the first time.

Brigit asked in disbelief, "You're taking that wooden boat of yours across the Race?" Everyone knew it was dangerous to take small boats with outboard motors through the current and high waves of the Race. "You could be lost at sea."

Albert smiled, "Don't worry. We won't be the only boat. There will be one other boat accompanying us."

For a minute Brigit felt a little better, but she couldn't believe Aunt Agatha wasn't more troubled, "Aren't you worried about them Aunt Agatha?"

"No, David is eighteen, and Albert is already twelve. They have spent summers on the beach since they were born. They are strong swimmers and know how to handle their boat. And, they each have a guardian angel to watch over them," Aunt Agatha said calmly as she handed them their morning orange juice.

Sipping her juice, Brigit walked back to the front door. Kevin O'Connell and his friend, Brendan Kearns, were carrying Kevin's boat down the beach. It was low tide. The sunrise was spectacular. A giant red ball of sun reflected red and orange colors across the eastern morning sky and the low tide waters of Long Island Sound.

"Red sky at night, a sailor's delight; red sky in the morning, a sailor's warning," Lillian said with a half smile. Brigit knew her mother was also hoping the boys would reconsider their voyage.

Brigit wondered out loud, "Are Kevin and Brendan going with you?"

"Of course, they are our best friends. Who else would go with us?" David answered. David and Brendan had grown up together not only summers in Baiting Hollow but also as classmates in their Richmond Hill neighborhood in Queens. What a pair. Brendan was tall, thin, and handsome with strawberry blonde hair, blue green eyes, and a sweet smile. David was not quite as tall as Brendan and had sun bleached blonde hair and clear blue eyes. Both boys were brown as berries from the summer sun. All the teenage girls swarmed around them when they walked down the beach. They were so cool.

Brigit's cousin, Albert, was also very

handsome, although he was a little shorter and more outgoing than his brother. He loved to tell stories and joke around. He always had a smile and made everyone else smile. The minute he walked in the room, the entertainment began. And, when Albert and Kevin were together, there was no stopping them.

Since no one else seemed concerned about the boys' safety, Brigit decided not to say another word. And, if, only if, Kevin's story was true, not only was he a descendent of merpeople, maybe all of her cousins were! She was stunned with the possibility but chuckled to herself at the lack of probability. "It is ridiculous," she thought. "But, I have to get to the bottom of Kevin's story. I will proceed cautiously, assuming his story is true. And, I do like that possibility."

Next thing she knew, Kevin and Brendan were knocking at the front porch door, "Good morning. Ready to go?" Brendan asked as the two boys opened the screen door and came in. Brendan had to lower his head a little as he walked through the door. Kevin told David and Albert that he and Brendan had already been to the gas station before dawn and bought all the gas they'd need for the ride across the Sound. "When we get to Connecticut, we'll find a marina to buy the gas we need for the trip home," Kevin reported on the game plan.

"We each better bring a change of clothes, towels, and sweatshirts, because it will probably be cold on the ride back tonight."

"Captain David," Brendan playfully addressed his friend with a salute, "Are you ready to ship out?"

David smiled, enjoying his new title, but realizing he and Brendan were not only responsible for themselves but also for his younger brother and their friend, Kevin. "Ready!" he saluted back, "Let's get my boat down to the water."

David's wooden boat was a little larger and much heavier than Kevin's boat so two boys could not carry it to the water. The four young men filed out the front door with all their things. Albert and Kevin ran under the bungalow for the four inflated rollers needed to move David's boat to the water. David and Brendan lifted the front of the boat as Albert and Kevin placed one roller under it and back about midway and the other roller toward the front. Then David and Brendan lifted the back of the boat, motor and all, so Albert and Kevin could place one roller about four feet in and one closer to the back end of the boat.

Brigit, her mom, and aunt watched from the porch as the four boys pushed, and the boat slid over the four rollers. Sliding backwards down the beach, one roller would be freed from the front of the boat. David and Brendan would hold the back of the boat up, so Albert or Kevin could put that roller under the back of the boat. Over and over they repeated this pattern until the boat slipped into the water. Kevin and Albert picked up the rollers, ran barefoot up and over the low tide exposed stones, placed the rollers under the bungalow, and ran back to the boat. They were so excited to be included in the older boys' adventure, that they would do anything for them.

As David jumped into his boat, Brendan ran down the beach to Kevin's boat, lifted the anchor, rolled up its rope, and put it in the boat. Standing knee deep in the water, he held the boat waiting for Kevin to join him.  As soon as Albert jumped into David's boat and Kevin jumped into his boat, motors were started.  With both motors idling, sputtering and smoking, the boys turned toward the bungalow.  Standing tall, proud, and handsome, they waved and threw kisses.  Aunt Agatha, Lillian, and Brigit waved back, threw kisses, and watched the two motorboats with the four Baiting Hollow beach kids head north across the sound to Connecticut.

Lillian and Agatha sat down on the wicker furniture and started to reminisce about their heyday as young adults at the beach.  Brigit stayed on the front deck until the two boats were specks on the northern horizon and then finally disappeared from sight.

Then Brigit slipped back into the porch and sat near her mother. The two sisters were so engrossed in their stories, they never noticed Brigit join them. How Brigit loved to be a fly on the wall and listen to her relatives tell stories about the good old days. But, today she had a new purpose for listening. She was hoping to hear something that might give her a clue to understanding the Twomey legacy.

The spell cast over Lillian and Agatha by their beloved memories was broken by a knock at the back door. "Hello! Is anybody home?" Aunt Clare called as she came in. The back screen door slammed behind her.

Aunt Clare was the youngest child of
Margaret and David Twomey's thirteen
children. Married to Uncle Frank and living
in East Islip with her two children, Leo and
Paul, Aunt Clare came to the beach to spend
a day with her sisters. It had always been
Aunt Clare's dream to have a family reunion,
and today she and her sisters were going to
begin making that dream come true.

Lillian, Agatha, and Brigit walked to
the kitchen to greet Clare. Hugs and kisses
were given to everyone. No sooner had
everyone settled back on the porch, than
Aunt Alice's and Aunt Mame's cars pulled
into the parking space behind the bungalow.
Brigit ran outside across the slate path

through the sand to their cars. Hugs and kisses again for everyone. "Can I help you carry anything from the car?" Brigit asked her aunts. Aunt Mame, the eldest Twomey daughter, had a bowl of her homemade potato salad for lunch and her bag with her bathing suit and towel for a swim. Aunt Alice, the second daughter of Margaret and David, was Brigit's godmother and a prize-winning cook from Sound Avenue.

Brigit followed her aunts into the kitchen of the bungalow. "We are out on the porch," Aunt Agatha called to her sisters. Brigit put Aunt Mame's potato salad and Aunt Alice's prize winning lemon meringue pie in the refrigerator and their beach bags

in the back bedroom. By the time she
returned to the porch it was packed with her
mom, four beautiful aunts, and her father
and sister who had just gotten up. Lillian
headed back into the kitchen to get coffee
and juice for everyone as Aunt Agatha told
about David's, Albert's, Brendan's, and Kevin's
excursion to Connecticut.

There were very few chores expected at
the beach. Every morning the beds had to
be made and the sand swept out of the
bungalow. Agatha and Lillian liked to cook
the meals and wash and dry the breakfast
and lunch dishes together. Brigit and her
sister set the table for dinner and did the

evening dishes. After a day at the beach and an ice cold shower on the back deck to wash off the salt and sand, everyone was suppose to hang their wet suits and towels on the clothesline that was strung from the deck to the post by the road. When you drove up to the bungalow, that old clothesline was a rainbow of flapping beach towels and bathing suits.

Brigit finished her few morning chores and decided to take a walk down the beach to the creek. On the way she picked up a few pieces of blue and green beach glass, one small white cradle shell, and a beautiful purple and gray wishing stone. She knew it was a wishing stone, because it had a gray ring around the center of the purple stone.

Brigit thought carefully about how she would word her wish.  Should she wish Kevin would tell her the truth?  If he did, would she ever completely believe him?  Should she wish her mother would tell her the secret of Baiting Hollow?  If her mother told her, she would be breaking her promise, because she already told Agnes O'Connell.  Brigit did not want to wish that on her mother.  Her only wish must be to find the Twomanno Pearls. She believed they were hidden at the Twomey farmhouse, and she knew her mother would want her to find them there. "I wish, I wish…," Brigit hesitated for a moment staring at the wishing stone she held in the palms of her hands.  She knew if her wish came true, it would change her life forever. But, she knew she must find out, "I wish I would find the Pink Twomanno Pearls at the Twomey farmhouse this week." There, it was done. Brigit clenched the purple and gray stone in her right hand, closed her eyes, and with one huge heave tossed the wishing stone into the water as she had heard from Kevin it must be done to seal the wish.

Walking back to the bungalow, Brigit saw her younger sister, Barbara, building a sand castle above the high water mark near the jetty. Brigit climbed onto one of the large gray boulders of the jetty and sat down to watch her sister. Her little sister was ten years old, only two years younger than

Brigit.  As Brigit admired Barbara's long red curly hair, sunburned fair freckled skin, and sea blue eyes she heard Barbara singing a little made-up song as she added pebbles and shells to her sand castle, "Tiny shells washed ashore, rest in sand and sun once more, journey's end or just begun... Beachcomber's treasures, such a find:  rare, unique, and undefined... child's toys on a sunny day, gathered in pails and carried away... young girl's jewels carefully placed on sand castles designed with style and grace... nature's beauties, little shells, tickle my mind with stories to tell."

As Brigit watched she had a flashback of Kevin's story, an image of Abigail on the rocky outcrops combing her long curly red hair and singing to lure the human death dragon ships, so they would crash. She could not believe how much Barbara resembled Abigail. If anyone was a mermaid, Brigit knew then and there, it was Barbara. She knew she needed help to find the pearls. She also knew Barbara was the best at keeping secrets.

Brigit stepped off the jetty, walked up to Barbara, and offered the sea glass and cradle shell for her sand castle. Barbara smiled, "Thank you, they are beautiful. I know just where to put them." Barbara placed them carefully on the fragile sand tower and stepped back to admire her work.

"There," she said and smiled very satisfied.

"It is beautiful. You are such an artist. I don't know how you do it. Everything you make, whether a sand castle, painting, soap sculpture, is always beautiful. Today, everyone on the beach will enjoy looking at your sand castle," Brigit said with her arm around her sister's shoulder. Then and there she decided, "It is final. I will tell the secret of Baiting Hollow to Barbara."

Brigit asked Barbara to come and sit on the jetty next to her. She asked her to make the promise she had made to Kevin the night before just a few feet away from where they were now sitting. Barbara closed her eyes and promised, and Brigit started to tell her the story. "In a time before time was conceived of, in a place not recorded on maps, off the shore of a ragged coastline, tiny merpeople emerged from the sea..." Barbara never interrupted Brigit's story telling.

By the time Brigit finished the story, the tide had come in. The two sisters were sitting on stones which were now almost completely submerged under water. "Let's ask Mom if we can go back to the farm and stay overnight with Aunt Mame and Uncle David," Brigit suggested.

Barbara nodded, her eyes as big as saucers, "But, what about the Twomey ghosts?"

"Don't worry," her big sister assured her. "They aren't real. Uncle David just made them up to keep us out of the attic and cellar. There are no such things as ghosts. I'll bet we'll find the Pink Twomanno Pearls in either the attic or the cellar."

As they entered the porch, the five Twomey sisters were finishing their lunch and Aunt Alice was sharing her first draft of "The Twomey Family Tree." Aunt Alice asked if the girls would like to hear what she had written. "Oh, yes!" both girls answered. They found a comfortable seat, and Aunt Alice started to read:

*To the best of my knowledge, I shall*

*try to present the facts of the "Twomey Family Tree." Some I can recall in my own lifetime. Others have been told by my family members and some by figuring according to the dates in the cemetery plot.*

*About 1850, there was a terrible potato famine in Ireland and many left the "ould country" and came to America to escape starvation. Since my grandfather, John Twomey, was born in 1843, I can imagine his coming to America, sailing from the town of Cork in Ireland, as a young man, possibly twenty years of age, the date being around 1863.*

*How Grandpa happened to come to eastern Long Island, I do not know, but he lived in Baiting Hollow at one time. That is where my father, David, was born..."*

"The pieces are starting to fit together," Brigit whispered to Barbara.

"Do you think Great Grandfather John Twomey and Grandpa Twomey were merpeople?" Barbara asked.

Brigit smiled, nodded, and whispered back, "Now, you are thinking. We'll figure out this secret before the end of the day."

Aunt Alice continued reading, *"My brother, Johnny, used to tell the story of how Grandpa Twomey happened to acquire the Twomey homestead and farm. Possibly in the latter 1860's..."*

After the story was finished, Brigit and

Barbara offered to clear away the lunch dishes, so the five Twomey sisters could go for a swim.

As the last of the dishes were brought from the porch to the kitchen, there was great laughing and talking as the sisters came out of the bedrooms, put their swimming caps on, and headed out the front door to the water. Brigit and Barbara watched them. They dropped their beach towels above the high water mark and walked right into the water. Like an Esther Williams water dance troupe, one, two, three, four, five swimmers dove in and started swimming to the raft. One, two, three, four, five swimmers hopped up on the raft. They sat with their faces toward the afternoon sun and rested as they were gently rocked by the waves.  Brigit and Barbara looked at each other and nodded.  "They are mermaids," Brigit said.

Barbara agreed, "Another piece of the puzzle."

Following their afternoon swim, Brigit and Barbara sat reading on the back deck of the bungalow outside the kitchen door. Brigit heard her mother in the kitchen.  She slowly walked to the screen door where she could see through to the kitchen.  Her mother was making dessert for dinner. Brigit stared at her.  She notice her apron bow neatly tied.  She watched her knead the pie dough.  As she picked up a handful of dough and began to form a ball to roll, Brigit noticed her mother's wedding ring covered with pie dough. Brigit remembered stories her mother told about Grandma Twomey's "simple wedding band." Her mother had one, and Brigit knew she wanted the same when she got married.

As her mother began to pour the blueberries into the pie shell, Brigit's thoughts again drifted to the farm. She thought about the wild blueberry patch in the woods at the far end of the potato field. She remembered picking blueberries last summer for Aunt Mame to make pie for Uncle David.

Brigit's mind started to remember many adventures and stories of her time at the farm. One day while taking a walk together, her mother told her about her horse, Pearl. She showed her where Pearl was buried by the side of the barn. Every summer part of the ritual when they'd arrive was to walk over by Pearl's grave. Could this be another clue? Brigit didn't know anyone else with a horse named Pearl.

Behind the barn was an old chicken coop. Brigit's mother had told her stories about gathering eggs. Brigit remembered the fun her sister and she had making a play house a couple of summers ago in the coop. Mame had given them an old tablecloth and some old dishes. Uncle David gave them an old table and two chairs from the barn. And, her mother helped them sweep out the chicken coop and pick wild flowers for the table.

The timer's ringing startled Brigit's attention back to the kitchen. Her mother was taking the pie out of the oven. Brigit opened the screen door and walked into the kitchen. The top of the pie was golden brown. The filling was still bubbling as her mother placed it on the hot plate. "Looks good," Brigit said, "smells good, too."

"I made it for dinner tonight, it's your father's favorite pie," her mother mentioned.

"Are Aunt Mame, Aunt Alice, and Aunt Clare staying for dinner?" Brigit asked.

"Clare and Alice had to leave early to make dinner for their families. They left while you and Barbara went for your swim. Mame is staying, but she will have to leave right after dinner," Lillian explained.

"Do you think Aunt Mame would let Barbara and me visit with her at the farm for a day or two?" Brigit asked her mother.

\*\*\*\*\*\*

Brigit, Barbara and Mame were just stepping out of the car at the farm when they heard the phone ringing. Brigit ran ahead

up the steps of the back stoop by the
honeysuckle bush, through the lobby, into
the kitchen. She liked the fact that the door
was never locked. It made her feel safe and
always welcome. She ran into the dining
room and then into the living room. At the
foot of the staircase was the phone stand.
Brigit loved Mame's old telephone. It was
something out of an old movie. Brigit
answered, and a man said, "Hello, is Mame
there?"

By then Mame arrived by the phone,
Brigit handed it to her, and Mame said
"Hello," as she sat on the bottom steps by
the enormous banister. Brigit remembered
what fun it was years ago sliding down the

banister with her cousins. Then Uncle David put a stop to it, because he said it wasn't safe, and someone may get hurt. Brigit thought that banister was so big and so strong it could hold the whole Twomey family at the same time.

Brigit went back to the kitchen where Barbara was rocking in the family rocking chair. It was the biggest wooden rocker she had ever seen. All across the top were carved lions' heads, and the arm rests and legs were carved to resemble a lion's paws. It was an awesome sight. Mame said it had been in the family as long as she could remember.

"Well girls," Mame started as she came back into the kitchen, "That was cousin George. His wife, Judy, is very sick, and he has asked if I would come spend the night. Uncle David has gone into the city to meet Uncle Chris at the airport. They are staying over night at Agatha's house in the city and driving back early in the morning. If you stayed here you would be all alone. Do you want me to take you back to the beach, and we'll have our sleep over tomorrow night?"

"O.K.," Barbara started to say as Brigit interrupted.

"We'll be fine here tonight, Mame. You're down the street and a phone call away if we need anything. We'll lock all the doors to be on the safe side, watch television and go to bed early," Brigit said.

Mame agreed. Being the eldest of the thirteen Twomey children, she had a lot of responsibility when she was twelve years old helping her mother take care of the babies and the house.

Brigit and Barbara brought their bags upstairs. Climbing the ancient staircase, they faced the door to the attic at the head of the staircase. They were not allowed to go up there without Aunt Mame. Uncle David said that the family ghost, Denny, lived in the attic. Usually, that was enough to keep the girls and boys out of the attic. "But tonight is different," Brigit thought. "Tonight, we're going up into the forbidden attic, Denny or no Denny."

At the head of the stairs, Uncle David's bedroom was on the right, and Aunt Mame's was on the left next to Uncle Chris's room and the bathroom. Brigit and Barbara turned left then right down the narrow hall. The nursery with two cribs was on the right. Beyond the nursery was the master bedroom, which was Grandma and Grandpa Twomey's. Further down the hall on the left was Uncle Johnny, Uncle Bud and Uncle Joe's old room. And, at the far end of the hall was the large room over the kitchen. Aunt Clare, Aunt Jerry, Aunt Peggy, Aunt Alice, Aunt Agatha, and Lillian had all shared this room from time to time.

Mame left for cousin George's around

eight o'clock, and the girls decided to take their showers and get ready for bed. They would search for the Twomanno Pearls when they knew there was no chance of any relatives stopping by for a visit. Sitting up on the big brass double bed in the room over the kitchen, the girls gabbed, put curlers in their hair, and gave each other manicures when Brigit thought she heard a noise in the attic. She wouldn't dare say anything to Barbara and dismissed it as the wind. As she finished putting her last curler in her hair she heard the noise again. This time it was a little louder and sounded like one of the old attic trunks with metal wheels rolling a short distance across the wooden attic floor. She took a deep breath and decided to ignore it again. Barbara hadn't said a word and had just finished putting on her nail polish. She asked Brigit, "Do you want me to put polish on your nails? You can have pink, red, or white polish."

As Barbara was painting Brigit's second hand, there was a thud in the attic above them. The loud, grinding, metal wheels slowly rolled across the attic floor. The two sisters sat up straight and stared at each other in silence. Two scared girls in shortie nightgowns, slippers, rollers, and wet nail polish sat frozen on the big brass bed in the Twomey farmhouse all alone. Or were they?

"Did you hear that, Barbara?" Brigit whispered.

"Yes," Barbara whispered back. "Did you hear it the other two times?"

"Yes! Oh, my goodness! Do you think someone is in the attic?" Brigit asked. She knew they couldn't go anywhere. The nearest neighbor was two miles down Twomey Avenue. There wasn't a phone at the bungalow, and she didn't want to bother Mame.

Barbara and Brigit cuddled next to each other up against the headboard, hugging their pillows. "Maybe someone came in this afternoon when Uncle David went into the city and Mame was at the beach," Barbara wondered out loud.

Brigit knew she had to take control of the situation and protect her little sister. "Do you remember, Barbara, how Abigail found her courage to lure the ships onto the rocks and to leave her merclan to find safety for her babies? We have to be brave and smart, too. Follow me."

Barbara nodded, jumped out of the bed, and tiptoed behind Brigit down the long narrow hall, past the attic door, down the creaky old staircase, through the living room and the dining room, past the parlor, and into the kitchen. She wasn't exactly sure of Brigit's plan, but Barbara trusted her big sister and would follow her anywhere.

Was she shocked when Brigit opened the utensils drawer in the kitchen, pulled out two huge butcher knives, and held them up in front of her. "If whoever is in the attic comes near us, we will have these to protect ourselves," Brigit told her sister. Brigit held out one large knife for Barbara to take. As Barbara reluctantly took hold of the knife, Brigit ordered her in a whisper, "Follow me."

Brigit led Barbara out of the kitchen, back through the dining room, past the parlor, to the living room holding their butcher knives out in front of them for protection. Brigit made sure every downstairs lamp and light was turned on.

"Let's watch television. Maybe the noise was just our imagination. A good television program will take our minds off our worrying," Brigit suggested to calm Barbara.

Brigit turned on the television as Barbara hopped up into Uncle David's favorite recliner. Brigit sat on the couch near Barbara. Late night cartoons came on. The two girls tried to force a smile, a giggle or two, and a laugh for each other, but inside they were scared to death.

A loud thud sounded above their heads followed by the sounds of chains being dragged across the ceiling. Wide eyed they stared at each other, butcher knives erect. Listening now not to the cartoons but to every clink and rattle moving above them. "Could someone have come out of the attic and gone into Aunt Mame's room?" Barbara asked. Brigit shrugged her shoulders, all out of leadership strategies and low on courage.

Brigit softly, stoically whispered to Barbara, "I don't think *somebody* is upstairs."

As the clink, clank, and rattle started down the wall, the two girls' eyes were as big as saucers. "My chest hurts. It is so tight. Are the Twomey ghosts haunting us?" Barbara whimpered.

Brigit knew something supernatural was happening. The knives were of no use to them now. She remembered Kevin saying that ghosts can't hurt you. Most people get so scared they end up doing something stupid to hurt themselves. She decided to try to calm Barbara down.

"Barbara, if they are Twomey ghosts, they can't hurt us. They are just teasing us. Aunt Mame said that Grandpa Twomey had a sister, Sarah. She was a terrible tease, always playing practical jokes on everyone. She wouldn't hurt us. We are family..."

BAM! A large, broad force hit the floor to ceiling window by Barbara's chair. "A-a-a-a-a!" Both girls screamed, and Barbara leaped from Uncle David's recliner to Brigit's lap.

"I'm calling Mame. Something awful

is happening!" Brigit said as she ran to the phone. Barbara held on to her from behind. The noises continued to echo around the room.

"Hello," Mame answered half asleep.

"Mame! You have to come home. Please, come home! Something terrible is happening. Barbara and I are scared to death."

"I'll be right home," Mame assured them.

No sooner did Brigit hang up the phone, then the noise softened. Brigit and Barbara went to sit in the kitchen with their butcher knives. The next five minutes felt like an eternity. Every few minutes or so the clink, clank, and rattle came through the kitchen walls.

Br-brum-brum, screech, a car pulled into the driveway. Brigit and Barbara ran to the window. It was Mame. As she came through the lobby into the kitchen, the two sisters cried and hugged their aunt, "We're so glad you're home."

"What is the matter?" Mame asked.

As the girls told the story of their frightening evening, they noticed the noises fade into the distant night. "Girls, that's just the fireworks in Riverhead. There are no ghosts," Mame assured them as she took the butcher knives from the kitchen table, washed and dried them, and placed them back in the utensils drawer. "How about a midnight snack? I have some homemade shortcake, strawberries I've defrosted from the June harvest, and real cream."

God Bless Aunt Mame. She knew how to make everything better. Aunt Mame fixed Brigit, Barbara, and herself bowls of strawberry shortcake swimming in real cream. As they sat at the table that evening in the kitchen, joy filled the Twomey farmhouse.

The two girls decided to sleep in the same bed that night, just in case of any more noises. "Aunt Mame is definitely a mermaid," Barbara said snuggled next to her big sister.

"There is no doubt about it," Brigit agreed.

\*\*\*\*\*\*

Brigit and Barbara slept late the next morning. The soft familiar mid morning farm sounds woke Brigit: the hum of the tractor working the potato field, the swish-swish of the irrigation system, the pick-up truck doors' opening and closing, and Uncle David's and Uncle Johnny's walking into the kitchen for their ten o'clock coffee. Next thing she knew, Uncle Joe and Uncle Chris were driving up and joining their brothers for a coffee break from the Twomey Mobile Service Station. Now that Uncle Chris was home from the air force, he worked there with Uncle Joe.

Brigit could hear cabinet doors open and close, cups and saucers assembled, and hearty laughter among the brothers. The coffee aroma and the smell of fresh baked bread filled the house. The sun was shining, not a cloud was in sight. It was a perfect beach day.

"Are we going to look for the Twomanno Pearls today?" Barbara mumbled as she rubbed the sleep out of her eyes.

"I don't think so. The fright we got last night, I think was intended as a warning to keep us from snooping around for the pearls," Brigit said cautiously. "We'll do our detective work somewhere else. Kevin should be back at the beach today. I'll ask him."

The two girls bounced down the stairs to the kitchen. After giving each of the uncles a good morning hug and kiss, the girls sat down to breakfast. Mame cooked up stacks of pancakes with butter and maple syrup. The girls watched Mame take a large slab of bacon from the icebox in the pantry and cut off several slices then fry them in her big black iron frying pan. Pancakes, bacon, fresh squeezed orange juice, and fresh baked bread was their favorite breakfast.

After doing the breakfast dishes, Brigit

and Barbara walked up the dirt road behind the house through the potato fields to the pump house. Her uncles and a few other men were refilling the pesticide tank attached to the back of their large red tractor. When everything was ready, Uncle David gave Uncle Johnny a wave. Johnny jumped back up into the seat of the tractor, turned on the engine, waved back, and drove into the field of potato plants to continue the spraying.

"Do you girls want a ride on the tractor back to the barn?" Uncle David asked Brigit and Barbara. Thrilled, they stepped up on the axle of the small gray tractor's huge back tires on either side of Uncle David. They stood on the axle covers, leaned against the metal fenders that partially covered the tires, and held onto the edge of the fender as Uncle David started the tractor engine. "Ready? Hold on tight, here we go."

When they arrived at the barn, the tractor stopped, and Barbara immediately jumped off. Brigit hesitated and asked, "Uncle David, you promised when I turned twelve you would teach me how to drive the small gray tractor. I've been watching you drive, and I think I could do it. Do you have time to teach me now?"

"Are you already twelve?" Uncle David smiled as he realized his little niece was growing up. "All right, a promise is a promise. Jump up here in my seat. Barbara, you'd better wait on the lawn."

Brigit was tickled pink. Over the years she envied her cousins as Uncle David taught them. But, she knew Uncle David always kept his promises, and her day to learn to drive the tractor had come. Uncle David moved over to the fender Barbara had been leaning against, and Brigit hopped into the driver's seat.

She paid close attention as he described the clutch, shift, and the gas and brake pedals. Uncle David coached her on how to drive the tractor, "Put one foot on the clutch and one on the brake pedal, move the shift stick into drive. Raise your right foot off the brake and gently place it resting on the gas pedal. Raise your left foot slowly off the clutch, while gently stepping on the gas." The tractor lurched forward. Barbara jumped back a little further into the lawn. "That's good," Uncle David said to encourage Brigit. He had taught all his nieces and nephews how to drive the tractor when they turned twelve years old. He was a good and patient teacher.

Brigit could not believe the tractor was moving. "Steer!" Uncle David reminded her. "Stay on the driveway. Let's drive up to the pump house." Barbara watched with pride as her big sister drove the tractor for the first time. She knew in two years Uncle David would teach her, too. She couldn't wait.

After dinner that night Uncle David told Mame he was going to feed the cows in the south pasture and then go water the geraniums on the Twomey graves in Saint John's Cemetery in Riverhead. "Can I come?" Brigit asked.

"Sure," Uncle David said. "Barbara, do you want to come with us?"

"No, thank you. I'll stay with Aunt Mame and help with the dishes. Then, she said we'd make sponge cake with chocolate frosting for tomorrow's dinner," Barbara answered.

Brigit followed Uncle David to the lobby where he sat on a stool and put on his work boots. He grabbed the watering can and handed it to Brigit, "You can take care of this." Then, Brigit followed him out to the barn. She watched as he opened the two massive barn doors. There was the big flatbed truck. Uncle David loaded several bales of hay onto the truck then opened the door to the truck cab and motioned to Brigit, "Jump in." Brigit loved to climb up into the truck and sit next to her uncle.

Uncle David backed the truck out of the barn, stopped, hopped out, closed the barn doors, and then hopped back into the truck. The first stop was the cow pasture. As the truck drove down Twomey Avenue, the black and white cows started heading for the gate. They knew it was feeding time. Brigit loved to see her uncle feed these beautiful animals. He gave a couple of pats on the heads of two or three cows, and Brigit did too.

At the cemetery, Brigit knew exactly where the water spigot was to fill the watering can. She had come here many times with Uncle David or Aunt Mame. She learned about her ancestors by the stories they told her as she followed them from grave to grave. Every year Uncle David and Mame planted red geraniums on all of the Twomey graves. They always paused at Loretta's tiny headstone next to Grandma and Grandpa Twomey. "Tell me again what happened to Loretta. Was she six years old when she died?" Brigit asked as she held the metal watering can to pour water on Loretta's geraniums.

Uncle David took a deep breath. He squatted down next to Brigit, pulled a few weeds that had grown around the geranium by the headstone, and started to tell Loretta's story:

*On Long Island in 1920, Mom and Pop raised thirteen kids. Pop farmed the land. Mom kept the home. They prayed to God for peace and love. One day while Pop was raking leaves into piles for autumn burning, little Loretta, only six, put down her rake and started dancing. Loretta leaped across the lawn. She held her arms up high above her. As she twirled, her skirt waved outward, her eyes cast upward toward the sky. Round and round Loretta was dancing, to and fro while Pop was raking. Loretta was floating, almost flying, in her world of sheer delight.*

*Suddenly, we heard her screaming, screeching, running, crying, calling. Her skirt was burning. The flames now dancing, streaking across the yard were a horrific sight.*

*Mom ran out with blankets flying. Pop ran too, his heart was pounding. Fear and fright ran right beside them to their little daughter's side.*

*We watched Mom meet Loretta and wrap her tiny burning body in blankets from our home. We watched Pop helping Mom.*

*He scooped Loretta in his strong arms and carried her into the house.*

     *Pop sent for the doctor to treat Loretta. Brothers and sisters sat beside her. Mom and Pop tended her day and night. We prayed to God for our lovely little sister. Ten days later, our precious sister, dancer, dreamer, gentle loved one, left our home for heaven above. Now, Loretta's with God the Father and Blessed Mother. Leaping, twirling little Loretta, angel sister, we will always love you.*

     Uncle David stood up, took Brigit's hand, and they walked to the truck.

******

Back at the farm, Mame asked Brigit and Barbara if they wanted to go to the grocery store with her. Since Uncle David was going to be around working in the barn with Uncle Johnny, the two girls decided to stay at the farm. Mame said she would be back in less than an hour.

"This is probably our last chance," Barbara said to Brigit as they walked up to the room over the kitchen. "I followed Mame into the attic while you were away. You wouldn't believe the things up there, and there was no sign of Denny. In the corner was a large brown trunk with leather straps. Mame said it was Mom's from college, and she wished she'd take it home with her.

Mame was trying to clean out the attic. Let's take a look in Mom's trunk.

Brigit had never disobeyed Uncle David or Aunt Mame, but she knew this was her last chance to find the Twomanno Pearls and to find out who she really was, "O.K., let's do it."

"Follow me," Barbara said with a smile, "After all, I know where the trunk is in the attic."

Everything seemed to move in slow motion. Cautiously, the two sisters tiptoed down the narrow hall. Barbara took hold of the glass doorknob, turned it, and pulled the door open. Barbara looked at Brigit with her eyes wide open. "Go," Brigit prodded.

One step at a time the girls climbed the attic stairs. It was dark, with only a sliver of light coming in through the rafters. Barbara reached up and grabbed the string hanging from the ceiling at the top of the stairs the way she saw Mame do that afternoon. Click, the light was on. Brigit surveyed the attic. "Over here, Brigit," Barbara pulled her arm to a dark corner. They had to stoop low to walk to the trunk. Then, they knelt down in front of their mother's college trunk, unlatched the leather straps, and slowly opened it. They just stared for a minute or two.

Folded neatly on top of everything was a yellow lace gown. Barbara took hold of the shoulders of the dress and pulled it out of the trunk.  She took a step backwards and held the gown in front of herself.  "Very pretty," Brigit commented then turned back to the trunk.  There was her mother's letter sweater.  "Did you know Mom was a champion tennis player in college?"

"No, that's really great," Barbara answered.

Under the sweater Brigit found her mother's Red Cross Life Saver's Certificate. Then she picked up a large sketchpad from college.  As she turned the pages she saw page after page of charcoal nude drawings. Brigit had mixed feelings.  She knew it was art, but it seemed a little immodest.  She quickly closed it so Barbara couldn't see it.

Brigit turned to see Barbara dressed in her mother's yellow lace gown. Holding the skirt up so she wouldn't trip, Barbara curtsied. Brigit stood up and met her with a bow. Then put one arm around Barbara's waste and took her right hand with the other. Barbara followed as Brigit led her sister in a fanciful dance around the attic. Banging her head on a low ceiling beam, Brigit said they'd better stop and get to work. They didn't have much time left.

While Barbara slipped out of the yellow lace gown and folded it back up neatly, Brigit went back to the trunk. It was full of so many treasures: college textbooks, photographs, letters, riding boots, etc...

Then Brigit noticed a faded tapestry pouch. She picked it up as Barbara knelt back next to her. Opening the pouch, Brigit pulled out a blue velvet jewelry box. "Could this be it?" she whispered.

"Open it!" Barbara pleaded. Holding their breath, Brigit opened the velvet jewelry box.

"Ah!" they both gasped. There in the box were two pale pink pearls. Each pearl was fastened to a small gold chain.

The attic silence was broken by Aunt Mame's car pulling in the driveway. "We better get out of here," Barbara yelled.

"Sh, sh," Brigit cautioned. "We have

to get everything back in the trunk the way it was. You go downstairs. Talk to Mame. Offer to help her bring in the groceries. Tell her about how much you want to learn to drive the tractor. Stall her! I'll clean up."

As Barbara ran down the attic stairs, Brigit took one more look at the two pink pearl necklaces. Then she quickly tucked the box in the tapestry pouch and placed it back in the trunk. After carefully putting everything else back in the trunk, she closed the lid, fastened the leather straps, turned off the light, and came down the attic stairs. She quietly closed the attic door and tiptoed back to the bedroom over the kitchen. Brigit lay across the big brass bed. Her heart was racing.  She needed to calm down and decide what to do next.

****** 

Brigit woke early the next morning but didn't want to get up.  She was so confused about finding the pearls.  She felt a little ashamed that she disobeyed her Aunt Mame and Uncle David.  And now, Barbara didn't want any part of the search for their true identity anymore.

Last night before they went to bed Barbara said that they had two close calls. The ghosts terrified her, and they almost got caught snooping in the attic.

She told Brigit to be satisfied she had found the pink pearls and to not include her in her detective work anymore. "I have a mother and a father who love me, and I have lots of relatives who love me. That's all I need to know," Barbara announced. Now, Brigit thought Barbara might be right.

Brigit heard a car pull up to the back door. Mame was out back hanging clothes on the line. "Hello, boys," Mame called out.

"Hi, Aunt Mame," Brigit heard two familiar voices call back to Mame.

She jumped out of bed and looked out the window. She thought to herself, "What were they doing here? If they think I am coming downstairs to visit dressed in shortie pajamas, they are crazy. I will pretend I am sleeping if Mame comes upstairs to call me."

Brigit peeked through the window watching Kevin, Brendan, and Mame talking. She heard a few laughs, then they each gave Mame a hug and a kiss and left in Brendan's car.

Mame came upstairs with the empty laundry basket. She poked her head into the bedroom. "You had some company this morning. Two handsome young men came to visit," Mame announced. "Kevin said he hoped to see you today, Brigit. He wanted me to give you the message to meet him on the jetty after dinner tonight. He said they had a great trip across the sound to

Connecticut, and he wanted to tell you all about it. Are you ready for breakfast?"

\*\*\*\*\*\*

After the dinner dishes were done and the bungalow swept out for the night, Brigit walked outside onto the beach. Kevin was nowhere in sight, and she was not going to sit and wait like some wallflower on the jetty. So, Brigit decided to take a walk to the creek. Climbing over the first jetty, she glanced up to the O'Connell bungalow. There didn't seem to be any activity there, so Brigit kept walking.

On the way back from the creek, Brigit

saw Kevin fishing from the beach in front of his bungalow.  He was so involved in his fishing, he didn't notice her walk behind him and climb up on the jetty.  The tide was changing, which Kevin always said was the best time to catch fish.  "Catch anything," Brigit called to Kevin.

"Not yet.  But, I am glad to see you," Kevin looked over in Brigit's direction, holding his rod steady in the water.  "Oh, I think I have a bite!"  Kevin reeled the fish in. It put up quite a fight.  When it finally came out of the water, both Kevin and Brigit realized it was a blowfish.  Kevin took the hook out of its mouth and threw it back into the water.  He picked up his bucket and threw the water in the sound.  He picked up his fishing rod and tackle box and said, "I'll be right back. I want to put my fishing gear in the bungalow."

While waiting for Kevin to return, Brigit decided she would let Kevin tell his story about the trip to Connecticut first. He seemed so anxious to share it. Then, she would tell her story about the two pale pink pearls Barbara and she found in the Twomey attic.

When Kevin came back, he ran down the beach, took off his sweatshirt, and threw it on the sand, as he said, "Let's go for a swim out to the raft." Kevin ran into the water and dove under before Brigit even stood up. Since she was always in her bathing suit at the beach, she dove from the jetty into the water, came up next to Kevin, and they swam together out to the raft.

Sitting on the raft, Kevin started to tell Brigit his story. "I couldn't wait for you to come back to the beach, so I could tell you what happened to us. I looked for you all day yesterday. Brendan and I stopped at your Aunt Agatha's bungalow this morning. I was so disappointed when your mother said you were still up at the Twomey farmhouse with Aunt Mame and Uncle David. Brendan said he would drive me up to the farm before he went to work, so I could see you. When we got there Mame said you were still sleeping, so I left her the message for you to meet me. I am so glad you came back. You will never guess what happened to us in the Race."

*After we waved goodbye to you, your mom, and your aunt, we headed north. It was easy to stay on course, because the sun was rising in the east. Brendan sat at the front of my boat navigating. We followed a safe distance behind David and Albert.*

*The northern horizon line was cloudy, so we couldn't see the Connecticut shore. A minute or so out, Brendan said, "I can hardly see Baiting Hollow." I turned around, and I couldn't see it at all. David and Albert were well ahead of us now, so I had to give my motor the gas to try to catch up. We needed to stay together through the Race.*

*What a beautiful day it was.  There was a strong wind and big gray and white clouds floating across the blue morning sky. Every once in a while Brendan would point out huge sailboats and fishing boats about to cross our path, schools of bluefish frantically breaking the surface of the water, and flocks of seagulls flying above.  It was a glorious start to the day.*

*David and Albert waited for us to catch up to them just outside the raging waters of the Race.  "Try to stay closer.  We have to move quickly through the Race," David yelled to us.*

*I thought to myself, "He better go a little more slowly.  My thirty-five horsepower*

Johnson Seahorse may not be able to keep up with his fifty horsepower Johnson, but my aluminum boat was stronger and safer any day than his wooden boat. I wasn't afraid, although Brendan looked a little pale. David put his motor in gear and waved us onward. I waved back to signal that we were ready.

What a ride! Five-foot waves pounded our boat from side to side. Once a ten-foot swell lifted us high above David's and Albert's boat. I waved and laughed. Brendan held on for dear life. His knuckles were white from holding on tightly to the sides of the boat.

"Yippee!" I yelled. It was like riding a wild stallion: up and down, back and forth *jerking this way and that. Waves' splashing over us, we were drenched. "Grab a bucket and start bailing some of the water out," I yelled to Brendan. With a huge gulp, he let go with one hand and grabbed the bucket. He did hold on with the other hand as he bailed the seawater out of the boat.*

*Next thing I knew we were in the valley of a fifteen-foot swell. I looked up, and this time David and Albert were riding the top of the swell. They weren't waving or smiling, neither were Brendan and I. Then, suddenly, the wave crashed over our heads. A wall of water engulfed us, and the last thing I remember was the bottom of David's boat coming down on top of us. Brendan and*

*I dove out of my boat and out of the way of David's boat.*

"Kevin," Brigit gasped, her eyes opened wide and her arms holding her knees up to her chest. "How did you guys survive that? Who saved you? How did you get home?"

"Be patient, Brigit," Kevin said calmly. "There is more to the story." And, he continued.

*Buried deep within the swirling waters of the Race, I didn't know which way was up. Just as I would seem to start rising, another huge pressure would force me tumbling down deeper. Then a strong undertow of some sort dragged me in what seemed like an* inescapable current. I knew you should never fight an undertow; you should just go with it until it releases you. So, I decided to ride it out. I actually wondered for a second if it was part of the Beluga Current that Daniel brought Abigail through to Baiting Hollow.

The water was dark. I couldn't see my hand in front of my face. I was worried about Brendan, David, and Albert. I could feel myself start to panic, so I said a little prayer to my guardian angel, "Angel of God, my guardian dear, please save Brendan, David, Albert, and me from the swirling tentacles of the Race."

In the cold darkness, I felt someone's

*arms around me. I decided it was my guardian angel rescuing me and fell into her arms. She swiftly whisked me to the surface.*

*I gasped, choked, and coughed. I felt very disoriented, but tried to look around to see if Brendan, David, and Albert were also being rescued. My eyes dashed far and wide, trying to spot a glimpse of my friends and our boats. I was startled to see a beautiful woman still holding on to me.*

"Brigit! It was Abigail!"

"Oh, my goodness, Kevin!" Brigit cried out, "That's wonderful! What did she say? Did she know where Brendan, David, and Albert were?"

Brigit slid over next to Kevin and with

both of her hands held tightly onto one of his hands, "You could have died out there."

Kevin put his other hand on top of Brigit's hands, "Listen Brigit."

*"Do not be afraid," Abigail assured me. "Daniel and the seven Guardians are rescuing your friends and setting your boat upright. David's boat was shattered by the force of the waves."*

*"We have been making as may trips as possible to Baiting Hollow these last few months to deliver merbabies to the women of Baiting Hollow," Abigail said sadly.*

*I asked her why there were so many more orphaned merbabies than before.*

*"Oh, Kevin, there are many reasons. It*

is with great sadness, I must tell you that the
merpeople are on the verge of extinction. The
mermaids and mermen who followed Lord
Lahranno to the deepest ravines of the ocean
are feeble and weak. Many have secretly
given their merbabies to Queen Daphnia
knowing they face a sure death beneath the
sea. Queen Daphnia turned her castle into an
orphanage for merbabies. The dolphins
guard them. They take them on daily outings
to the seashore. There, they play on the rocks
and in the tidal waters the way we did years
ago. She is using the chest of Pink
Twomanno Pearl, which Queen Twomanno
gave her just before she past away. Queen
Twomanno had predicted this disaster to her

dear friend, Queen Daphnia. Queen Daphnia promised her she would do everything she could to ensure the merbabies safe passage to land."

"Queen Daphnia got word from the dolphins the other day that a spy told Lord Lahranno about the merbabies' orphanage. He now plans to attack the castle with an outlaw band of sharks he has organized to capture the merbabies. Queen Daphnia has asked Daniel, the Guardians, and me to work day and night to take these babies to Baiting Hollow. We must make one more trip to deliver the last two merbabies to Baiting Hollow. It is there only hope."

"Kevin, there is another reason,"

Abigail told me.  "The ocean is dying!"

"What?"  I shouted back in disbelief.
"What do you mean, the ocean is dying?"

"Kevin," Abigail informed me, "The
dolphins and the whales who live under the
sea are endangered because of the selfish
human greed and ignorant disregard for the
beauty and delicate balance of nature.
Whales and dolphins are hunted and
slaughtered or sold to theme parks. Millions
of tons of garbage, chemicals, and sewage
are dumped into the ocean everyday. The
polluted waters are choking the plants and
animals under the sea. And now, the brown
tide is headed toward your Long Island
Sound. When the brown tide comes, the

*dolphins will not longer be able to swim in the sound. Daniel and I must hurry to bring the last two merbabies here before the tide arrives."*

*I had so many questions to ask her, "Abigail..."*

*"I must go now, Kevin," she interrupted. "Meet me at the jetty in two days after tomorrow, just before dawn. I would love to see your sister, too. This will be my last trip to Baiting Hollow. After we deliver the last two merbabies, Daniel, the Guardians, and I must go into hiding. Lord Lahranno has a bounty on our heads. He has vowed to stop us and make us pay for taking the merbabies to land. He blames us for the imminent extinction of the merpeople."*

*Abigail wrapped her arms around me and kissed me, I imagined the way she did the night she gave us to Lillian twelve years ago. She said, "Good-bye, Kevin. I will see you in three days."*

*With a wink and a smile she dove away. Her beautiful green, silver, and blue tail flipped high, sparkled in the sunshine, and slipped into the sea.*

*Just then, I heard my boat's motor coming behind me. I turned to see Brendan, David, and Albert waving and calling to me. David and Albert reached out to me and pulled me into the boat. It was so good to see each other. We hugged each other and cried with relief and joy.*

*"You wouldn't believe what happened to us," Albert started explaining. "There must have been seven or eight dolphins who came out of the blue to save us. We grabbed hold of them, and they brought us to the surface. To our surprise, your boat, Kevin, was floating on the surface. Unfortunately, David's boat was shattered. As soon as we got into the boat, the dolphins swam away."*

Brigit, I never told the other guys about Abigail. I just knew they wouldn't understand, and I felt it was part of the secret of Baiting Hollow.

*Well, we couldn't believe how the waters had calmed around us. As the sun was setting, we decided to head back to*

*Baiting Hollow and not continue our trip to Connecticut. We had had enough excitement for one day.*

"I am so grateful you are safe," Brigit said hugging Kevin.

"Brigit, will you meet me at the jetty just before dawn? Can you sneak out of the bungalow?" Kevin asked.

"I will, Kevin," Brigit emphatically answered. "Nothing could keep me from meeting Abigail. And," Brigit paused, "You need to know that Barbara and I found the Pink Twomanno Pearls in the Twomey attic last night. I wasn't sure you were telling me the truth, and I had to see the pearls with my own eyes and hold them in my hands.

Oh, Kevin, they were so beautiful. Now I believe you, and I will never doubt you again."

\*\*\*\*\*\*

Brigit sat up all night in her bed on the porch of the bungalow. She kept one eye on the small travel alarm clock by the side of her bed and one eye on the jetty watching for Kevin to come outside. The sky was so beautiful, a full moon and millions of stars. The night waters of the sound reflected millions of silver sequins of light.

At about three o'clock in the morning, Brigit saw a dark silhouette walking along the jetty. She knew it was Kevin. Brigit carefully stepped out of her bed and walked out the front screen door and down the steps to the beach. Kevin was watching. He waved when he saw her. She waved back and ran to him.

Brigit and Kevin walked out to one slate gray stone of the jetty just past the high water mark. Surrounded by water they sad side by side holding each other, waiting for Abigail.

The stars were out in full glory. The full moon painted a speckled path of light across the dark blue-black waters. Suddenly, the moonlight spotlighted a dolphin leap out of the water, pause, and dive back into the sound. Kevin and Brigit expected to see seven more dolphins follow in suit. There was no sign of the Guardians. "I wonder what happened? Where are the Guardians?" Brigit whispered.

"Something's wrong," Kevin whispered back to Brigit.

With their eyes focused, hearts pounding, toes twitching, the two beach kids sat frozen like statues on the jetty. "I hope Abigail, Daniel, and the babies are all right," Brigit sniffed.

Kevin pointed into the water. Just beyond the jetty there was a large shadow underwater. Kevin and Brigit held their breath.

SWISH! Right before their eyes,

Abigail leaped out of the water and settled on the jetty. In her arms were two little sacques. Abigail opened the sacques, checked the babies, hugged and kissed them, and seemed to look beyond Kevin and Brigit. It was as if she did not even see them there. Brigit and Kevin knew they were witnessing a sacred moment.

From behind them, they were startled to hear a familiar woman's voice, "Hello, Abigail." Kevin and Brigit turned to see Brigit's mother standing next to them.

"Hello, Lillian," Abigail said to her dear friend. She hugged the merbabies, kissed them, and handed them to Lillian. Lillian took both babies and hugged and kissed them the way Abigail had.

"Lillian, these are the last merbabies. My dear friend, this is the last time I will see you. After Daniel and I find a way to save the Guardians, we will go into exile far from Lord Lahranno. Thank you for your devotion to the merbabies. Queen Daphnia wanted to thank you for your love and commitment for the last fifteen years. Queen Daphnia has proclaimed you, Lillian, the Queen Mother of all land living merpeople. She has commissioned a mural to be created on her castle walls depicting you accepting merbabies by the Baiting Hollow jetty. Historians are writing the history of the merpeople. They have recorded the many trips Daniel, the Guardians, and I have made, and your name is always there on the pages of our story.

Queen Daphnia gave me the last Twomanno Pearl. She wanted me to use it to join the human race and be safe from Lord Lahranno's vendetta against me. His sharks have already captured and imprisoned the Guardians, and now they are after Daniel and me. But, I can't. I belong to the sea. Daniel and I will stay and live in the ocean. Please take the last Twomanno Pearl as a gift from Queen Daphnia and me.

Lillian begged her, "Please, Abigail, please live with us. You are so much a part of our family. I know Al and the children would welcome you. Abigail, you have trusted me to take care of your babies and many orphaned merbabies. Trust me now to love and take care of you. I love you as a sister. Please, come live with me and be one of my sisters."

"Thank you, Lillian. I will always think of you as my sister. You will always have a special place in my heart. But, I cannot leave Daniel. Daniel and I must find a way to save the Guardians and free the merpeople. And, the sea is my home, Lillian. You must know I am a hundred years old. In the sea, I am young and vital. Renewed everyday by the saltwater, kelp, seaweed, and sunshine. If I used the Twomanno Pearl to become human, I would be a one hundred year old woman, with one hundred year old legs. My hair would turn gray, my skin would wrinkle, and my bones would atrophy. The sea gives me life," Abigail explained as she looked out toward the water. The moonlight sparked on a little tear falling from her blue eyes as it slid down her cheek.

Lillian took two steps through the water to Abigail with the babies in her arms. Abigail put her arms around Lillian. The world stood still as the two friends shared their love for each other.

Then, Abigail dove into the sound to meet Daniel. Kevin and Brigit waited and watched. Up, out of the water, high above them Daniel rose with Abigail sitting high on his back. She waved, threw kisses with both hands, and they silently disappeared into the water.

As Kevin and Brigit turned around to say something to Lillian, she was gone. A sliver of light on the eastern horizon signaled the start of a new day. The marsh birds began to chirp, a flock of seagulls flew off the cliffs, and fishermen backed their boat into the water.

******

There were only two reasons beach kids had to wear shoes, if they were going to town or to church. Today was Sunday. So, Brigit and Barbara reluctantly wore their calico sundresses and white sandals.

During mass, Brigit prayed for the angels to be sent to help Abigail and Daniel save the Guardians and the merpeople. She knew the many stories her father told about how the angels guarded, protected, and enlightened people on Earth.

Brigit prayed that the angels would somehow enlighten Lord Lahranno, free him of his fear, and have him trust in the goodness and beauty of nature. Brigit prayed, "Please, send angels to defend the merpeople, protect them against the wickedness of Lahranno, help Abigail and

Daniel free the Guardians..."

Back at the beach, Brigit did not join her family for Sunday brunch. Barefoot again, wearing only her blue and green swimsuit, Brigit walked outside.

During the week, Baiting Hollow belonged to the beach kids, but on Sunday, it seemed as though the whole town of Calverton and part of Riverhead came to the beach. Below the high water mark, families, teenagers, and babies sat on blankets and beach towels. An occasional beach umbrella and ice chest interrupted this colorful patchwork. The water between the jetties were decorated with inflated black truck tire tubes, multicolored vinyl tubes, beach balls, and individual rubber floats. Children and adults played with an assortment of beach toys: pails and shovels, whiffle bats and balls, volleyballs and nets. Brigit decided to take a walk to the privacy of the creek.

At low tide the creek was barely a trickle. Brigit walked across and continued to the foot of the great cliffs. Alone now, she walked out into the water until she was waste deep, dove in, and swam to a gigantic boulder exposed by the ebb tide. She climbed up onto the north side of the boulder and rested. The sun was hot, the air humid, and the water still. Brigit rested and fell asleep.

Awaken by the cold sound water now covering most of the boulder, Brigit noticed the late afternoon sun. She gazed far down the beach and saw that most Sunday beach visitors and their paraphernalia were gone. She decided to swim back to the bungalow, since the current would be with her.

Approaching the jetty, Brigit noticed Kevin on the raft waving for her to join him. Brigit hopped up. "You were gone for quite a while. Are you all right?" he asked.

"I'm all right, just a little tired and sad. Kevin, we have to do something to help Abigail and Daniel. I just don't know what. I prayed for them in church this morning."

"Brigit, after I left you this morning, I went to bed. I slept most of the day and had a series of terrible nightmares about Abigail,

Daniel, the Guardians, the merpeople, and Lord Lahranno. Then, something strange happened. An angel came to me in my dream and told me to tell you that we must meet him at Queen Daphnia's castle Wednesday at sunset. We must wear our Twomanno Pearls. Wearing the pearls into the water, our bodies will return to mermaid and merman forms. This is the only way we can make the journey from Baiting Hollow to the castle. The angel said he would give us courage and guide us on the journey," Kevin paused to see what Brigit's reaction would be.

Brigit smiled and put her head on Kevin's shoulder, "I know we both have our guardian angels. Abigail has been so wise.

Daniel is so brave and strong. The Guardians are loyal friends. They need us now. Alone we are powerless, but with the protection and inspiration of the angels to guide us we must fulfill our legacy. The peace and beauty of the ocean must be restored. This will only occur if we overthrow the reign of Lord Lahranno." She sat up straight and tall, "So, Kevin, what's the plan?"

"Well, I don't have every detail worked out," Kevin scratched his head and looked away for a minute thinking. Brigit waited confidently. She knew that Kevin knew more about the ocean and the coastline than a master cartographer. "First things first. Tonight, we have to get our pearls. We need a good night sleep.  We'll meet at the jetty just before dawn tomorrow.  We have to leave before the fishing boats head out.  Wear your pearl around your neck.  Then, we'll play it by ear.  We'll say our prayers, follow the Beluga Current along the Grand Banks of Newfoundland.  I think we can pick up the Gulf Stream to cross north of the Mid-Atlantic Ridge.  We have to stay north of this ridge, because I've heard there are a lot of underwater volcanoes and quakes with lava spewing from them.  The Gulf Stream should bring us to the Celtic Shelf off the southern coast of Ireland.  From there I know the sea creatures will help us find our way," Kevin ended confidently.  He put his arms around Brigit and kissed her on the forehead.  "I need you by my side.  I can't do it alone.  Brigit, we'll take care of each other, and our angels will protect us."

Fortunately, Brigit's family always goes to the Twomey farmhouse on Sunday evenings for dinner.   Aunt Mame makes a big dinner and relatives from all over Long Island come to visit, eat, talk, and reminisce. Brigit loved to sit quietly in the corner of the big farmhouse kitchen and listen to stories her relatives told about her ancestors coming from Ireland, settling on Long Island, buying the farm, building the farmhouse, growing up on the farm, and the many pranks her mom's brothers and sisters used to play on each other.

Tonight would be different. Brigit would have to slip away from her relatives and go into the attic without anyone noticing. This time she would be alone. This time she would have to sneak up into the attic with a houseful of relatives. It seemed impossible, yet Brigit knew she had to do it. She had to get her Twomanno Pearl. She knew her mother would want her to have it.

\*\*\*\*\*\*

As Kevin and Brigit approached each other in the darkness of early morning, they

each noticed the moonlight reflect on their
pink pearls, which hung around their necks.
They stared knowing they were going to
embark on an adventurous journey, and yet
knowing they were going to be safe. The
courage of their ancestors and relatives and
their faith made them stand tall and proud.
Without a word, Kevin took Brigit's hand,
and they walked out onto the jetty and dove
into Long Island Sound.

The two beach kids were on a mission.
With the guidance, protection, and help of
the angels, they were going to save Abigail,
Daniel, the Guardians, and hopefully, free
the merpeople. It wasn't until they noticed
the shadow of a ferry boat overhead that

they paused and looked at each other. They both smiled with delight at their new forms and kept going. They knew they had to be out of the sound before sunrise to avoid the fishermen and their nets and lobster traps.

Brigit and Kevin joined a school of whales as they headed up the coast of Cape Cod. The sun was rising now. Kevin and Brigit were tiring, so they surfaced to rest for a moment. "Kevin, I don't' know if I can make it," Brigit said as tears welled from her eyes.

One of the whales spoke, "My name is Arthur. Get on my back, and I will carry you. My family is headed to the Grand Banks of Newfoundland then through the

Gulf Stream. We will bring you safely to the Celtic Sea. You will be safe with us."

Kevin and Brigit were speechless. They thought that the whales were sent to protect them. They held onto Arthur as he had directed and trusted he would bring them safely to their destination.

The ride was long. The ocean was wild. They swam through hurricanes with high winds, sea swells, and churning waters unlike anything they had ever seen in the sound. Arthur and his family swam through night storms. Thunder and lightening rocked the sky and the sea.

At sunrise on Wednesday, Kevin noticed the ocean seemed to calm, "Brigit, I think this is the Celtic Sea."

"You are right, Kevin," Arthur answered. "The water here is too shallow for my family to safely swim. You and Brigit must swim north through the Irish Sea."

"Is it safe?" Kevin asked.

"You must swim deep within the sea. Avoid all ships and stay away from shore. You must not be seen by man. It is safer than the open ocean, because Lord Lahranno's school of sharks is combing the ocean along the western coastline for Abigail and Daniel. They would never expect a mermaid or dolphin to swim into the Irish Sea. Swim through the North Channel, past the Giant's Causeway on the north coast of

Antrim.  Be very careful here.  Then, swim
west to the Rockall Trough.  Queen
Daphnia's castle is in the Rockall Bank
about two hundred miles northwest of
Ireland.  The waters are part of the Iceland
Basin and too cold for sharks to swim in.  I
will tell all sea creatures to watch for you.
Be brave, be wise, be safe," and Arthur
turned and left Kevin and Brigit in the Celtic
Sea.

"Are you ready, Brigit?" Kevin asked.

"I'm as ready as I'll ever be," Brigit
answered.

"Let's go!"  Kevin led the way with a
deep dive.  The two merchildren swam along
the floor of the Irish Sea and the North
Channel for safety as Arthur had instructed.

When the water started to turn colder, Kevin and Brigit knew they were approaching the Iceland Basin. Kevin waved to Brigit to surface. "We're safe, Brigit," Kevin exclaimed and hugged Brigit.

"For now," Brigit answered in a more serious tone.

Just then, an old dolphin greeted Kevin and Brigit, "Well, hello. My name is Seamus. It has been years since I've seen merpeople swimming freely in the ocean."

"We're..." Kevin tried to answer.

Seamus interrupted, "Wait, don't tell me. Could you be the two orphaned children of Abigail? The sea creatures are all talking of your arrival."

"Yes, we are. I am Kevin, and this is my sister, Brigit," Kevin answered. Brigit was surprised and pleased with Kevin's introduction.

"Oh, I remember the day Abigail brought you two to Queen Daphnia. I am the castle gardener. I took Abigail to visit the Queen. I remember being there as Queen Daphnia blessed Abigail, Daniel, the Guardians, and the two of you as you left for your new home on land. Does Abigail know you are here?" Seamus asked.

"No," both children answered.

"We have come to help Abigail and Daniel free the Guardians and overthrow Lord Lahranno. It is the only hope for the survival of the merpeople," Kevin explained.

"Follow me, I will take you to Queen Daphnia.  She will help you," Seamus directed.

Approaching Queen Daphnia's castle, Brigit said to Kevin, "It is more beautiful than I ever imagined."

As they entered the foyer of the castle, Kevin said, "Look, Brigit!"  Kevin pointed to artists' painting the mural Abigail told Lillian about.  "There is Baiting Hollow.  It seems so far away."

"Kevin, there's my mother and Abigail on the mural.  Do you think the two babies are supposed to be us?"  Brigit asked.

Seamus smiled, "Of course. If you look through the windows of our library, you can see the historians writing the story of the merpeople. It looks as though you two are going to be part of a new chapter, a new beginning for the merpeople."

Before they knew it, Seamus was leading Kevin and Brigit through the massive doors into the grand hall of the castle. Seamus spoke to another dolphin and then told the merchildren, "Wait here." He left with the other dolphin.

When they returned Seamus said with a smile, "Queen Daphnia has been expecting you," and led them into her ballroom.

As Kevin and Brigit followed Seamus,

they were overwhelmed by the grand ballroom: pillars of coral, floors of gold and silver, stained sea glass windows, towering cathedral ceilings with paintings depicting Zeus, Neptune, dolphins, merpeople, and many other sea creatures.

And, there on the thrown in front of them was Queen Daphnia, herself, surrounded by the four angels. Kevin and Brigit fell to the floor in humility to be in the presence of the royal messengers and protectors and the Queen of All Dolphins. The great hall was silent until Queen Daphnia spoke, "Arise children. Come to me."

Timidly, Kevin and Brigit approached the Queen. "You have become everything your mother had hoped. You are brave, strong, and wise. You have certainly remembered your legacy to protect the beauty and peace of nature. Your faith, hope, and love are pure. Through your prayers, the angels were sent to help in our time of need."

Queen Daphnia continued, "Last night, four angels came to me. They told me of your prayer and your trip across the ocean to save Abigail, Daniel, the Guardians, and the merpeople. Their message is that your prayers have been answered." Queen Daphnia raised her royal scepter, conch shells sounded, and through the grand ballroom doors came Abigail, Daniel, and the seven guardians, and they took their place in the ballroom.

"How...?" Kevin gasped.

Queen Daphnia raised her right had, conch shells sounded again, and through the grand doors hundreds of mermaids and mermen silently swam into the ballroom and took their place among the royalty.

"But, I thought..." Brigit interrupted.

Queen Daphnia nodded to her guard, and he once again opened the grand ballroom doors. Into the ballroom came an angel with Lord Lahranno swimming by his side.

"Ah!" Brigit and Kevin gasped in disbelief.

Queen Daphnia beckoned Lord Lahranno and his angel to come stand next to her. Then she motioned for Abigail to come sit next to her. When Abigail was seated, she looked to Queen Daphnia. Queen Daphnia nodded for Abigail to speak.

"Thank you, Kevin and Brigit. Through your courage and love you have saved the merpeople from extinction. Angels came as messengers to Lord Lahranno last night. Their words calmed his fears. Their message was a promise to take care of us, and they ask only that we in turn love and take care of each other. This is the only way the merpeople and all people and creatures of the Earth will survive."

Abigail continued, "Kevin and Brigit, Lord Lahranno and I are your parents from the sea. You also have adoptive parents on the land in Baiting Hollow. Your angels are taking care of all of us. Thank you."

Queen Daphnia spoke, "Kevin and Brigit, Abigail and Lahranno along with the merpeople and dolphins want to show their gratitude for your bravery. On behalf of everyone gathered here, I would like to crown you our new Prince and Princess of the Oceans." After a coronation ceremony, Queen Daphnia asked Kevin and Brigit, "Will you live with us and teach us about the faith, hope, and love which brought you back to us and saved us?"

There was a long, silent pause. Kevin and Brigit looked at each other. Then, Brigit spoke, "We all have been blessed. We have so much to be grateful for. Kevin and I feel privileged to be here and honored to be given the crowns of the Oceans."

Brigit looked to Kevin, "Thank you, all of you, for believing in the gifts of faith, hope, and love. Brigit and I are overwhelmed by the goodness in this room. We love you all very much, and that is why we came to help. But, our home is on the land. Our parents, waiting for us in Baiting Hollow, have loved and raised us selflessly since we were orphaned. We love them. We have large extended families and great friends we can not leave."

Kevin paused and then continued, "There is much work to do on the land. The faith, hope, and love you have learned are lessons that we need to spread on land. Fear, greed, anger, and selfishness must make way for love, kindness, peace, and joy. Brigit and I must return to Baiting Hollow, to our family, relatives, and friends and to our legacy to bring peace and beauty to the world. Thank you for your love and kindness to us. We will never forget you. We will always love you."

Queen Daphnia spoke, "As you wish. You will be written in our history books and depicted in our art as hero and heroine of the oceans, Prince Kevin and Princess Brigit. Know every sea creature will always love you. Please, come visit us often. You have my pledge to assist you in your work on land. Call on me if ever you need help."

Abigail swam to her merboy and mergirl, "I am so proud of you both. Whether you swim in the morning, during the day, or at night, I will always watch over you." She kissed and hugged Brigit. Then she kissed and hugged Kevin. "My beautiful merbabies, I will always love you. Daniel, the seven Guardians, and I will escort you back to Baiting Hollow."

******

Saturday morning Brigit awoke in her bed on the front porch of the bungalow. The sun was rising on a new day. This day, Brigit's family was returning to Connecticut. Her two-week summer vacation to Baiting Hollow was over. Her memories of these two weeks would be with her always.

Brigit could hear her parents' talking in the kitchen. "Instead of driving around the Long Island Expressway," her father was saying, "I thought we'd take the Orient Point Ferry to New London. What do you think, Lillian?"

"That sounds like a great idea. I'll call for a mid-morning reservation," Lillian said and headed next door to ask Agnes

O'Connell if she could use her phone.

For the next hour the family was busy packing their belongings into the station wagon for the ride home. Brigit took her bathing suit and beach towel off the clothesline. She put them in her suitcase with her shortie pajamas, slippers, bathrobe, Sunday dress, white sandals, books, and a small bag of shells, stones, and beach glass she would take home to her bedroom in Connecticut. She put on her jeans and T-shirt but decided to carry her sneakers and socks. Under her T-shirt, Brigit wore her pink Twomanno Pearl. She held on to it for a minute and promised herself she would never take it off.

Brigit asked her mother if she had

time for one more walk to the creek. This was Brigit's annual good-bye summer ritual. She picked up a few more stones and shells and dipped her toes into the creek for the last time. As she turned to head back, her mother was on the front porch waving her on. Brigit ran all the way back to the bungalow.

As she passed the O'Connell's bungalow, she noticed Kevin's boat was gone. She knew he must be out fishing with Brendan. Brigit remembered their good-bye the night before and knew they would see each other again next summer. She ran up the steps into the bungalow, grabbed her suitcase, and headed out the back door to the family car.

******

That September Brigit turned thirteen and started eighth grade.  While sitting in her science class the first day of school, she thought of one of her father's poems:

### Ready to Study

*Our footprints etch the meadows*
*And strips of golden beach*
*Rolling hills and hidden valleys*
*Masked in oak and silver beech*
*We gather pinks and lilies*
*Planted rows of infant pine*
*Listened to a nightingale*
*And trailed the porcupine*
*We're ready now to study*
*Really learn the triple R's*
*But a bit of us still wanders*
*Beneath the summer stars.*

All of a sudden, she heard her teacher Say, "The oceans are dying. The dolphins and whales are endangered..."

Without thinking, Brigit blurted out, "Are the mermaids all right?"

*****

ISBN 141200051-3